Polly
Neuro & the Cephalic Crew Friends
"The Vagus Nerve Super-Highway"

Polly Vagale

By Dora Henderson, LMHC-S, RPT-S, CST
Illustrated by Caitlynn Henderson, Carmen Luciano & Heather Worley

Hello!

I'm Dora, a play therapist who loves neuroscience and helping others to understand how our brain works in family-friendly ways! A huge shout-out to Dr. Porges for his Polyvagal Theory gift to the world. Dr. Porges work is a major inspiration in my therapy practice. My Neuro & The Ception Force Friends series was created to teach children and families different ways that our bodies gather information and respond to cues of safety and danger. Teaching us ways we can regulate, be more mindful and aware!

I would like to take this opportunity to share some very special thank-yous

for those who encouraged me throughout this project.

To my husband, Darryl Henderson for all your love and support.

To my mom Sylvia Edmark, you are my muse.

To my daughter and artist Caitlynn, for bringing my vision into reality through your artwork.

To my son, Brandon Henderson, for all your support.

To Carmen Luciano, my Business & Creative Development Specialist.

And a special dedication to Giraffe...

your genius & inspirational support is truly a blessing.

Dr. Steve Porges—for truly representing Safety & Connection.

Special thankyou for " adopting " Jackie Flynn & me —

The Neuroscience of Play Therapy Summit

at the Beach gals.

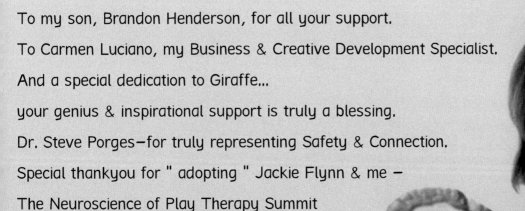

Neuro & the Ception Force Friends
are always on parade.
Your very own team of receptor neurons,
our work will never fade!

Down in Vagal Valley,
there is so much going on,
deep within your nervous system,
that helps to keep you strong.

I'm Ms. Polly Vagale, the teacher for
the Ception Force Friends band.
I'm stepping up to let you know
how I take command.

Deep down in Vagal Valley, inside of everyone you know,

there is a nerve that helps you learn and really grow.

Our Vagus nerve, problem solves and helps you regulate,

so much information in our world is really great!

Our Vagus nerve can be really busy

or at times really slow.

So that's when I step in

to help you go with the flow.

I manage your super-highway, which is the Vagus nerve!

The Ception Force Friends help you balance from within

when your life hits a speed bump or a bouncy curve!

When you feel lost, sad or when you're shutting down,

I can see that you're on Dorsal Vagal Road

where you have slow energy and often frown.

You don't want to always play with others

and might want to take a nap or be alone.

It's ok to travel down Dorsal Vagal Road and feel this for a

bit and then you will work with your Ception Force Friends

to help you balance lickety-split!

On Dorsal Vagal Road our Ception Force Friends

can step on the gas to boost you up.

Extero might help you to breathe deeply

by smelling a yellow buttercup, or

get your tastebuds zooming

and try eating a spicy tomatillo, or

maybe move your body to bring back your

energy with Proprio and Equilibrio.

When you feel alarmed and want to run or fight,

I can see that you're on Sympathetic Street

where you have high energy and your body is wound up tight.

You might be jittery, anxious, or a bit snappy,

not able to focus and really not happy.

It's ok to travel up Sympathetic Street and feel this for

awhile, then you will work with your Ception Force Friends

to help you stay safe and regulated, bringing on a smile.

On Sympathetic Street your Ception Force Friends
can help pump the brakes to calm you down.
Thermo lets you know to chill out
when you're fired up and having a breakdown.

Our body sends out signals for Intero to read,
relaxing you and helping you to regulate with super-speed.

When you get hurt Noci helps you through the pain
and then you're calm and able to really use your brain!

When you're feeling calm and connected,

you know that you're on Ventral Vagal Road,

where you're loved, safe

and protected.

When you travel through Ventral Vagal Road,

it's good to stay, play and then you will glow!

It's easy to talk to people here and share your feelings,

the best part of the Vagus nerve super-highway!

As we drive through Vagal Valley,

it's important to slow down and observe.

I pump the brakes or press the gas

to help you through every bump or curve!

Learning how to take care of your body and mind,

means discovering when to make a pitstop, to pause, and fuel

up so no feelings or thoughts are left behind!

Anger, sadness, or other big, big feelings

are a part of you and me.

Shifting between your thoughts and feelings is ok,

I think you can agree.

Neuro & the Ception Force Friends

let you know what your body might need.

You can choose how to respond to yourself or to others

and then on Vagal Valley you will proceed!

You can call a Ception Force Friend

to help you get on the road again.

They will always lend a helping hand

Getting you un—stuck again and again.

In Vagal Valley, we will keep you strong

See if you can notice us as your day goes along.

Neuro & the Ception Force Friends

are always here for you!

Keeping you safe and regulated

is how we shine through!

A special note to clinicians, educators, caregivers, & parents

My Neuro & The Ception Force Friends Book Series & Curriculum was created to present neuroscience in a playfully simple format in order to teach children how their body & brain communicate keeping them safe, secure, & connected.

Polly Vagale is a character that helps to teach children about their nervous systems through the lens of Polyvagal Theory, as she introduces this framework for all of The Ception Force Friends. Polly's explanation of the nervous system will help kids identify with their feelings, guiding them into self-regulation.

Our nervous system has receptors all over our body, sending information to our brains. For example, our receptors respond when we meet our favorite person & when that message hits our brain...we feel happy & our nervous system leads us to smile. The vagus nerve calms & excites our entire body automatically, & is important in the regulation of our emotions, behaviors, & sensations.

I enjoy seeing children gain a deeper awareness of their minds and body. May you enjoy your journey with Neuro, Polly & The Ception Force Friends Series and Curriculum. Dr. Steve Porges Vagal Theory rocks!!

Dora Henderson

Made in United States
Orlando, FL
16 December 2024

56025502R00015